MAMMALS

A TEMPLAR BOOK

Published by Granada Publishing 1985
Granada Publishing Limited
8 Grafton Street, London W1X 3LA

ISBN 0-583-30788-4

Devised and produced by Templar Publishing Ltd
Old King's Head Court, Dorking
Written by AJ Wood
Illustrated by John Gosler and Fran Stevens
Designed by Mick McCarthy
Typeset by Templar Type
Printed in Spain

GRANADA

Introduction

It is surprising just how many mammals there are for the young naturalist to study. Small ones like voles and shrews, predators like foxes and stoats, large placid mammals like deer – all have fascinating lifestyles and often leave signs of their activities for the nature watcher to find.

This Nature Notebook is packed with useful facts that will help you to find these animals and understand more about how they live. Every time you see one, tick the special box by its picture or fill in the notebook section. You'll also find lots of interesting projects to do and panels to fill in with your own nature notes. So whenever you're out and about, keep your Notebook with you and write down what you see.

Hedgehog

Contents

Garden mammals

If you want to see some mammals, one of the best places to start is in your own garden or the nearest park. Lots of the creatures that live there may be shy of humans and so keep themselves hidden away in the undergrowth. Others are nocturnal, which means they only come out at night. But you should be familiar with the grey squirrel shown below for it is common in gardens and parks almost everywhere. Squirrels are agile climbers and fast runners, bounding over the grass in search of fallen nuts and other tit-bits. Watch how they run up the trunks of trees, gripping the bark with their sharp claws. In the winter they build a special nest of leaves and twigs, called a drey, in which to shelter until the warmer weather arrives in spring.

◀ Look for the wily **fox** during early evening or whilst you're driving along in a car at night. You might catch sight of one crossing the road or disappearing into the undergrowth. It will probably be out hunting for small mammals such as voles and rabbits, although town foxes also raid dustbins to eat the scraps that we have thrown away!

The **hedgehog** is a friendly little ▶ creature, despite being covered with lots of sharp spines. It is common in gardens but only comes out at night so you may not see it very often. It eats all kinds of different food, from beetles and worms to scraps left out for birds! In the winter it curls up in a snug nest of leaves and grass and hibernates until spring.

Project

Meals for mammals

If you have a squirrel or hedgehog that regularly visits your garden, try putting out some food especially for them. Squirrels like nuts and seeds. You can buy a mixture of these from most pet shops. When the squirrel comes to feed, watch how quickly it removes the shells of nuts with its sharp teeth. Hedgehogs eat all kinds of

Squirrel food

scraps. You can see some of the things it likes below. Bread and milk is another favourite. If you stay up late one night you may even see the hedgehog come to feed. Which food does it like best? Record your sightings in the spaces below.

Hedgehog food

Who came to feed?

NAME _____

DATE _____

NOTES _____

_____

Voles & shrews

Scurrying quietly through the undergrowth at the edge of your garden there may be one of the small mammals shown below. The shrew, at the top of the picture, is always on the move, hunting out its next meal of an insect or worm. It has to eat nearly its own weight in food every day just to keep alive. The bank vole, at the bottom, is very common in country gardens where it lives on nuts and berries.

Common shrew

Bank vole

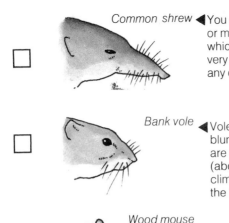

Common shrew ◀ You can tell a shrew apart from a vole or mouse by its long, pointed snout which is covered in whiskers. It has a very loud voice and will squeak loudly at any other shrew that invades its territory.

Bank vole ◀ Voles are chubbier than mice, with blunter faces and smaller ears. They are good climbers and weigh so little (about 1 ounce) that they can easily climb along bramble stems to reach the berries.

Wood mouse

◀ The wood mouse has large ears and a very long tail. Although more common than voles and shrews, it is seldom seen since it only comes out to hunt for food at night.

Project

Out and about at night

One way of finding out what small mammals are living in your garden is to record their footprints! You can do this quite simply with some stiff card, some soot, some cooking oil and a bowl of breakfast cereal.

Put the card on the ground near some undergrowth, such as a thick hedge or overgrown flower bed. Put a pile of breakfast cereal in the middle of the card and then surround it with a ring of soot mixed with cooking oil. Do this in the early evening and then leave your 'footprint trap' overnight.

In the morning you may find that some small creature has visited the food during the night. To get at it, the visitor will have had to walk over

the soot mixture which will have stuck to its feet and left footprints on the card. You might find vole or mouse prints on your card. To attract shrews you really need to use a bit of cat food.

Looking at footprints

Some of the most obvious clues to the mammals living in your neighbourhood are the footprints that they leave behind! Look for them in mud, along woodland tracks or at the edges of ponds and streams, and also after a fresh fall of snow in winter. Not all footprints are easy to identify. Large mammals, such as deer, leave quite distinctive tracks, but small mammal prints, like those of the mouse, shrew and vole, are harder to tell apart.

Fox prints show four toes, all with prominent claw marks. The middle two toes are much further forward than those on the outside. Dog prints can look quite similar but are usually wider and squarer than those of the fox.

Fox

Fox trotting

Dog

Deer tracks, called slots, are one of the easiest prints to identify, although they can sometimes be confused with those of sheep. Sheep tracks, however, have one half of the print larger than the other. With deer, both sides are equal.

Deer

Deer walking

Sheep

The squirrel's tracks are easily recognised. They show the four toes of the small front feet and the five longer toes of the hind feet. Sometimes the squirrel's trailing tail leaves a line through the middle of the tracks.

Squirrel

Squirrel jumping

Hedgehogs have five finger-like toes on both their front and back feet that usually show up clearly in their prints. If you find a line of hedgehog tracks, the front and back prints will often overlap.

Hedgehog

Vole

Front foot   Back foot

Shrew running

▲
The shrew's footprints are very similar to those of other rodents such as mice and voles. All of these small mammals have four toes on their front feet and five on their larger back ones. Their tails often leave a thin line.

Footprints I found

See what footprints you can find next time you're out on a nature walk. Write the names of the animals to which they belong in the spaces below.

1 _____

2 _____

3 _____

4 _____

5 _____

6 _____

Project

Making a plaster cast

If you find an interesting footprint in some muddy ground, you may like to make a plaster cast of it. To do this you will need a strip of cardboard, some plaster of Paris, paper clips and a bowl and spoon.

1 Once you've found your print, carefully brush any dead leaves or other debris away from it. Then surround the print with a ring of cardboard, as shown. Secure the ring in place with your paper clips.

2 Using the bowl, mix the plaster of Paris with some water until it is thick and creamy. Then carefully pour it into the circle of card until the print is completely covered and the plaster is about 3cms deep. Leave it to dry for about 20 minutes.

3 When the plaster is hard, dig up the whole thing and wrap it in newspaper. When you get home, carefully remove the card and wash the cast free of mud. You will find your print shows clearly on the bottom. Label it with the name of the animal and the place where you found it. The print shown here belongs to a badger.

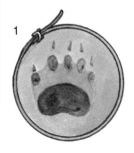

1

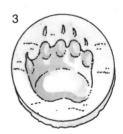

2

3

More mammal clues

Apart from footprints, many mammals often leave behind other signs of their presence. The grey and white hairs of badgers or the chestnut hairs of the fox sometimes get caught up on barbed wire fencing, for example, and the droppings of mammals like rabbits are easy to find on open grassland. Food remains are also a tell-tale sign that some small mammal has been feeding close by. Look for nuts and cones like those shown below next time you're out walking in the woods. You might even find them in your garden if you have a hazel or pine tree growing nearby.

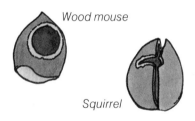

Wood mouse

Squirrel

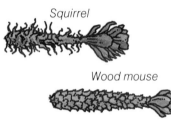

Squirrel

Wood mouse

These two hazel nuts have been broken open by two different mammals. The wood mouse gnaws a neat round hole in the nut shell in order to reach the tasty kernel inside. You can see this in the nut on the left. The squirrel splits the nut in half instead, using its strong sharp teeth.

Both wood mice and squirrels gnaw off the scales of spruce cones to reach the tasty seeds inside, but you can see that the mouse leaves a much tidier cone. If you find a cone that has had its scales peeled back, rather than removed, it is most likely to have been eaten by a bird.

Animal signs

Make notes about any animal signs you find in the spaces opposite. You could even start your own collection of food remains in an old shoebox. Label each of your 'finds' with the name of the animal that you think has eaten it.

FOOD REMAIN _____

ANIMAL _____

DATE _____

PLACE _____

NOTES _____

_____

Nature Notebook

Here are four mammals that you might spot in your garden. As you see each one, colour in the outline and fill in the spaces with your notes.

NAME   *Bank vole*

DATE

PLACE

NOTES

NAME   *Hedgehog*

DATE

PLACE

NOTES

NAME   *Grey squirrel*

DATE

PLACE

NOTES

NAME   *Fox*

DATE

PLACE

NOTES

Woodland mammals

Woods offer a rich habitat for many mammals. You may see squirrels clambering amongst the branches overhead or catch sight of a fox slinking out of sight into the undergrowth, but most of the mammals that live in the woods keep themselves well hidden. Badgers, like those shown below, often make their underground homes (called setts) in woodland. They come out at night to hunt for earthworms and beetles and will also raid the nests of bees to get at the honey! Opposite, you can see two other mammals that live underground.

Anyone at home?

Next time you visit your local woods, see if you can find a badger's sett. You can tell it apart from the den of a fox or a rabbits' warren by looking for the following signs.

1 The sett will have a number of entrances, a few metres apart, which are often dug into a bank or sloping ground. The holes will be about 30 cms (12 inches) wide.

2 You may find some of the badgers' black and white hairs caught around the entrances or on trees and bushes nearby.

3 Elder bushes may be growing nearby, for the badgers eat these fruits and deposit the seeds in their droppings.

4 You may find a tree growing near the sett which has deep scratches in its bark near the bottom of the trunk. The badgers will use it regularly to clean and sharpen their claws.

5 Close to the main sett you will usually find at least one latrine area. Badgers are very clean animals and deposit their droppings in shallow pits.

6 There may be piles of freshly dug earth in front of the entrances and also well-trodden paths leading away from the sett.

◀ The **marmot** lives underground in a complicated system of burrows which are lined with grass and leaves. Strangely enough, it is closely related to the squirrel which spends most of *its* time high up in the air amongst the branches!

Like badgers, **rabbits** live in large ▶ underground homes called warrens. Look for them in grassy places in fields and meadows and also on common land. You might see the rabbits feeding nearby at dusk.

Young badgers are born early in the year and usually stay with their parents until they are a year old. Some continue to live in the same sett, whilst others go off to find new territories. They are very playful creatures, often chasing and jumping on each other outside the sett.

Flying in the forest

The big old trees so often found in woods provide ideal living quarters for several species of bat. These small mammals are a little like flying mice for they have similar furry bodies and many have quite pretty mouse-like faces. Their wings are really modified hands that have a thin membrane of skin stretched between each of the long fingers. Bats are the only mammals that can truly fly, coming out at night to catch their prey of moths and other insects whilst on the wing. Below you can see three bats that often live in woods.

◀ The **Natterer's bat** lives in well-wooded country and parkland all over Europe, roosting in hollow trees and caves. Like many bats, the females bear only one baby each summer which can fly after just a few weeks. Natterer's bats can live for as long as 25 years!

The **pipistrelle** is one of the most ▶ common European bats. Groups of these pretty mammals can be found in woods and also in buildings where they find warm roosting places behind tile-hung walls and weather boarding! They are one of the smallest species, with a body that measures only 3-4 cms.

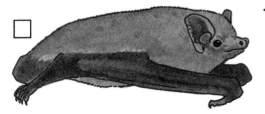

◀ The **noctule** is a large and powerful flier which can often be seen hunting insects before dark. These bats roost in colonies in hollow trees and can sometimes be heard squeaking in their tree trunk homes on hot summery days.

It might look uncomfortable to us, but all bats like to sleep upside down, hanging onto the surface beneath with their hooked claws. Often, great colonies of bats will roost together in hollow trees, caves and even the attics of houses. When darkness falls, the bats leave their roosts to go on a night-time hunt for insects which they catch by echo-location – sending out a series of high-pitched squeaks which bounce back off objects and work in a similar way to the radar scanning systems used on ships and aircraft. The squeaks are too high for us to hear, but you might see the bats themselves flitting about in the night sky during summer.

Thumb

Modified fingers

Wing membrane

Hind foot

Tail

Project

Making a bat box

You may be able to attract a bat family to your garden by supplying them with a home. Bat boxes are very similar to bird boxes and can be made in much the same way from a simple plank of wood. There are three things to remember before you start. First, the entrance is a narrow slit in the bottom of the box which should be no more than 2 cms wide. The small body of the bat can easily squeeze through. this gap.

Secondly, both the outside and inside of the box should be grooved so that the bats have no problem gripping to the surface. You can do this by running a saw over the surface, but ask a grown-up's permission first.

Thirdly, the box should be positioned high up in a tree and on the south side of the trunk so the bats will be warmed by the sun. If you do get some bat visitors, remember not to disturb them or they will fly away to another roost.

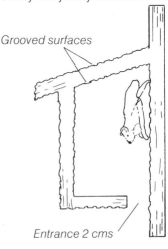

Grooved surfaces

Entrance 2 cms

Different deer

The largest mammals that you are likely to see in the woods are the deer. There are many different species, some of which are shown below. Only the males grow antlers – bony growths on their heads which are replaced each year. They are used for fighting in the mating season.

Deer generally feed on grass and other vegetation, standing on their back legs to reach the leaves and shoots of tall trees, but they will also eat crops and nuts like acorns or beech mast in the autumn. You might also see these beautiful creatures in both town and country parks and they sometimes stray into gardens in rural areas.

◀ The **red deer** is one of the largest wild deer in Europe, living in ancient forests and on highland moors. The males, called stags, are fine looking creatures with many-pronged antlers which they use during the breeding season to fight other stags. They can also be heard roaring at this time of year, making a loud bellow which rings through the forest to attract females (called hinds) and warns rival males of their presence.

The **roe deer** is the smallest native deer ▶ in Europe. It often lives in small groups deep in the undergrowth and can be seen feeding during the day in quiet country areas, its brilliant chestnut coat gleaming in the sun. Like other deer, the males use their small antlers to rub against tree trunks during the mating season to scent-mark their territory. This is called fraying. Look for small trees that have had their bark rubbed off – it may mean that deer are living nearby.

Look for **fallow deer** in country parks as  well as woodland. They have been kept in herds by man for many hundreds of years and those that live in parks are often tame enough to eat food from your hand. Fallow deer come in many colours, from milky white to almost black. Normally, they have bright chestnut coats covered with white spots in summer, and plain grey-brown coats in winter. You can easily tell them apart from other deer by their distinctive tails which are longer than those of other species and have a black line running down their middle.

◀ The **elk** is the largest of all the deer and can be found in North America and Asia as well as Europe. You can distinguish it from other species by its huge broad antlers. The elk spends its days browsing on vegetation in northern forests, especially round rivers and lakes. It will often wade into the water and duck its head down under the surface to search for the tasty stems of water lilies and other aquatic plants.

Young deer, called **fawns**, usually ▶ have spotted coats which help them to hide in the undergrowth, unseen by predators such as foxes. After a few weeks they are able to follow their mother but still return to hide amongst the bushes and other vegetation during the day. Most fawns are suckled by their mothers until they are a year old.

Watching mammals

Watching mammals can be a most rewarding hobby. The best time of day to go watching is in the early evening, just as it is getting dark. Whatever you are watching, remember to keep very still and quiet for nearly all mammals will run into hiding if they realise you are there. They also have a strong sense of smell so you must position yourself downwind of them or your scent will give you away. Apart from keeping still and quiet, the greatest asset of any young naturalist is ... patience! You may have to wait many hours to catch sight of a shy mammal, but when you do the wait will be worthwhile.

◀ Binoculars are very useful for watching creatures that you cannot get very close to – herds of wild deer for instance, or timid rabbits. You can wear them on a strap round your neck when out walking but remember to keep them in their case when not in use or the lenses may get scratched.

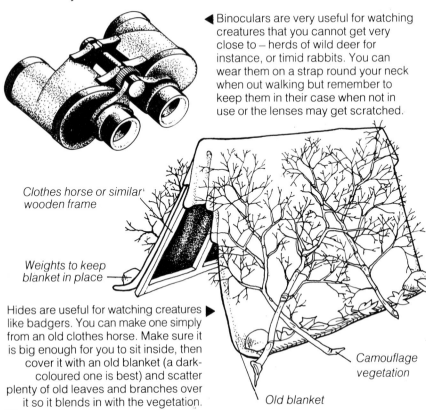

Clothes horse or similar wooden frame

Weights to keep blanket in place

Hides are useful for watching creatures ▶ like badgers. You can make one simply from an old clothes horse. Make sure it is big enough for you to sit inside, then cover it with an old blanket (a dark-coloured one is best) and scatter plenty of old leaves and branches over it so it blends in with the vegetation.

Camouflage vegetation

Old blanket

Nature Notebook

Here are four mammals you may be lucky enough to spot in a local wood or park. Remember to take a note of what each animal was doing and the time of day when you saw them.

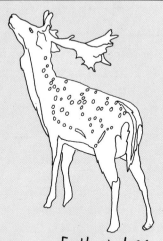

NAME ___Bat___

DATE _____

PLACE _____

NOTES _____

_____

NAME ___Fallow deer___

DATE _____

PLACE _____

NOTES _____

_____

_____

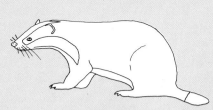

NAME ___Roe deer___

DATE _____

PLACE _____

NOTES _____

_____

NAME ___Badger___

DATE _____

PLACE _____

NOTES _____

_____

In fields & meadows

Somewhere near your home there is probably some open ground – a farmer's field perhaps or some common land. Such places are the homes of many different mammals, but the most familiar are undoubtedly the rabbits. These sociable creatures live in large underground homes called warrens. They come out to graze early in the evening so if you know where there is a warren nearby, stay up one summer evening and watch them feeding. Every now and then you might see one sit up on its back legs to check for signs of danger. If alarmed, it will warn its neighbours by thumping the ground with its hind feet and flashing its white tail as it runs for safety.

The **hare** is similar to the rabbit in many ways and from a distance the two can be difficult to tell apart. However, hares are much bigger than rabbits and have longer, black-tipped ears and powerful hind legs that enable them to reach speeds of nearly 35 miles an hour! Unlike rabbits, hares don't live underground.

Rabbit report

If you find a warren, pick a nearby spot where you can sit and watch the rabbits feeding one evening. Fill in the spaces below with your notes.

MY WARREN _____

DATE _____

PLACE _____

NOTES _____

_____

_____

_____

Mammals and their homes

Many mammals make permanent homes, like the rabbit's warren, in which to live and rear their young. Other creatures, like the hare, have no real home and spend their days crouching low in the grass or scrub waiting for darkness to fall. Even when its young are born, the hare makes no real nest. Instead, the baby hare, called a leveret, lies in a shallow depression made amongst the grasses. This is called a form. Some other animals also have special names for their homes or nests – a few of them are listed below.

Badger	Sett
Bat	Roost
Beaver	Dam
Fox	Earth
Hare	Form
Mole	Fortress
Otter	Holt
Squirrel	Drey

Hedgerow mice

Many different kinds of mice live in our woods and hedgerows, and in our fields and meadows. They are mostly shy little creatures who keep themselves tucked away amongst the grasses or undergrowth, searching for insects and berries on which to feed. The dormouse on the opposite page, spends half the year asleep underground. Only when the warm summer weather arrives will it come to the surface and build its ball-shaped nest of grasses amongst the undergrowth. You can tell it apart from other mice by its bushy tail.

◄ The **wood mouse** is common almost everywhere and is quite happy living in fields, gardens, town parks and hedgerows as well as woodland. It eats all kinds of food, from blackberries and other fruits to insects, snails and seeds. Its large hind feet enable it to leap out of danger rather like a kangaroo and it can move very fast, running and bounding along with its front feet tucked up out of the way.

The **harvest mouse** is one of the ► world's smallest rodents, weighing only a fraction of an ounce. Like the dormouse, it builds a small ball-shaped nest high up amongst the grass stems of fields and meadows in the summer. Harvest mice have very long tails which they use to grasp stalks and stems as they climb amongst the grasses.

Project

Finding small mammal bones

Occasionally, you may come across the carcase of a small mammal. Shrews, particularly, are often killed by domestic cats who will not eat them because of their unpleasant taste. You can clean up the bones by hanging the carcase in a jar of tadpoles. They will pick off any remaining flesh to leave you with a clean skeleton. Another way of finding mammal bones is to look for owl pellets beneath large trees or around farm buildings. The owl cannot digest the bones and fur of mice, voles and other prey so it spits them out as furry grey-brown pellets. If you find one and tease it apart, it will probably contain the broken-up skeletons of several creatures.

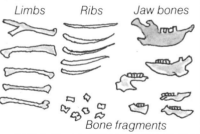

Limbs   Ribs   Jaw bones

Bone fragments

The underground mole

Look at any stretch of open land in the spring or summer and you may see a familiar molehill pushing up between the grass. You will be lucky to ever see the creature responsible, though, for the mole rarely ventures above ground. It spends almost all of its life tunnelling through the soil, searching for its favourite food of earthworms. It may occasionally poke its pink snout above ground to drag down old leaves and grass for its nest or to search for insects when food is short, but it is ill-equipped for life in the open, having very poor sight with eyes only as big as a pin-head!

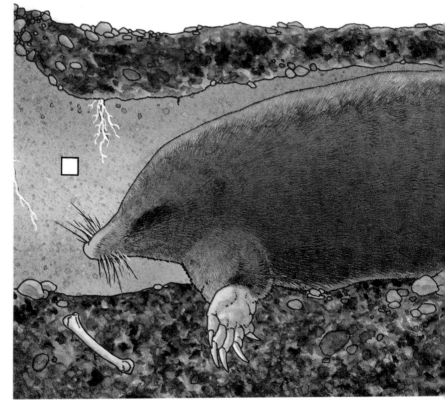

The mole's tunnel

The mole is continually extending its underground home. It digs and digs and digs, sometimes ending up with a tunnel system that covers over 1,000 square metres! As it burrows along, the mole pushes up the displaced soil as a familiar molehill. These mounds of earth are not used as entrances to its tunnel, though, and you can tell them apart from the anthills which are also found in grassy places because the soil will be loose and fresh.

Apart from the corridors along which the mole trundles in its search for food, it also makes a special fortress in spring to cover its nest chamber, rather like an extra-large molehill. Here, four or five pink and naked young are born in April or May. After about a month they are ready to leave and make tunnels of their own.

Molehill

Fortress

Corridor

Nest

Designs for underground living

The mole is well equipped for its underground way of life in several ways.

● Its broad front paws are perfectly designed for digging, with big strong claws and muscular shoulders that enable it to move its own weight in soil (nearly 8oz) every minute.

● Its paws are also covered with very tough skin to cope with all that digging!

● Its velvety black fur will lie backwards or forwards so the mole can easily run backwards down its tunnels without getting jammed. Its fur is also water repellant.

● The mole's nose and tail are covered with sensitive whiskers which help to detect any obstacles in its path. It also has touch sensors on its nose so it can find its way – and hunt down food – in the dark.

● Moles need to eat a considerable amount of food each day, a problem which they overcome in times of shortage by keeping a food store. The mole will collect a number of earthworms and bite their heads off so they cannot crawl away!

Stoats & weasels

When driving along a country lane, you may have seen a long, slender creature dash across in front of you and disappear into the hedgerow. This wily creature was most likely a weasel out hunting its prey of voles and mice. Weasels can be found in most habitats but are seldom seen, so good are they at avoiding contact with man! There are many other members of the weasel-family and, as you can see from the pictures below, they all share a similar shape.

The **stoat** and **weasel** look much ▶ the same but the stoat is bigger and always has a black tip to its tail. Unlike the weasel it turns white in winter. Both creatures are fierce hunters and are quite capable of killing animals like rabbits which are almost twice their size.

Here are three more of the weasel's relatives. The **ferret** is a domesticated form of the polecat which comes in many colours. The **polecat** is common on farmland and will often take over abandoned rabbit burrows as a home. The **mink** was introduced from North America for its fur. Like the ferret, it escaped from captivity and now lives in the wild. ▼

Stoat ☐

Weasel ☐

Ferret ☐

Polecat ☐

Mink ☐

Nature Notebook

Here are some of the mammals that you may come across in the hedgerows and fields. As you see each one, colour in its outline and fill in the spaces with your notes.

NAME   Rabbit
DATE
PLACE
NOTES

NAME   Mole
DATE
PLACE
NOTES

NAME   Weasel
DATE
PLACE
NOTES

NAME   Wood mouse
DATE
PLACE
NOTES

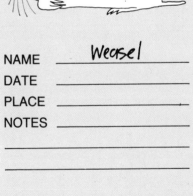

Water-loving mammals

A great many mammals spend all of their lives on dry land and although some are good swimmers when they need to be – the mole, for instance, or the fox – they do not choose to always live near water. On the next few pages you can see some of the creatures that spend their lives living in and around our ponds and rivers. Others, like seals or whales (which are mammals and not fish as you might think) spend most of their time in the waters of the sea. Just as the mole is specially adapted for its life underground, so these aquatic creatures have special characteristics to kit them out for their watery way of life. You can read about some of these in the panel below.

Webbed feet and flat tails

Aquatic mammals have adapted to their watery life in several ways. The otter, for example, can slow down its heartbeat whilst swimming underwater so that it uses up less oxygen and does not need to return to the surface so quickly.

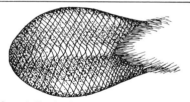

Specially-designed tails can also help animals to be more efficient swimmers. The beaver, which is found in mainland Europe, uses its broad flat tail like a ship's rudder to steer itself one way or the other.

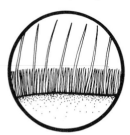

Many mammals have special fur, made up of two layers. The bottom layer is made up of short, dense hairs which trap air around the body to keep the creature warm. The long outer hairs act as further protection making the coat almost waterproof.

Many aquatic mammals have webbed feet which act in just the same way as the flippers worn by deep sea divers, to propel the animal faster through the water.

The **otter** is one of the most beautiful and friendly creatures to be found along our rivers and streams, although sadly it is now quite rare. Swimming up and down its stretch of river, the otter hunts for fish and other tasty morsels, sometimes stopping to dip and dive just for fun. Otters are playful creatures and excellent swimmers. They often use river banks as slides down which they can slip into the water. The otter's home, called a holt, is usually well hidden in a bank, often under an overhanging tree. Look for its droppings or spraints on your next riverside walk.

Living by the river

Here you can see two water mammals, the muskrat and the coypu, which are often mistaken for the otter on the previous page. The otter is a faster and more efficient swimmer however, and is much larger. The muskrat and the coypu were both introduced to Europe from America for their fine fur, but some escaped and set up colonies in the wild. They are most common on rivers with well-vegetated banks. The brown rat can be found in many different habitats apart from river banks but it is a good swimmer and can sometimes be seen swimming after food thrown to ducks and swans.

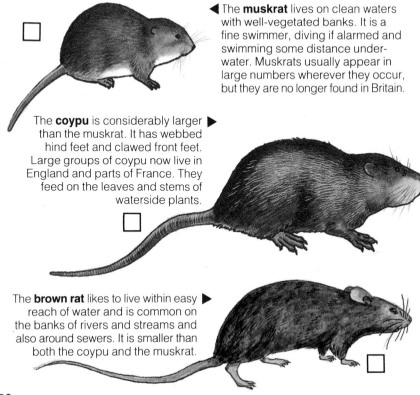

◀ The **muskrat** lives on clean waters with well-vegetated banks. It is a fine swimmer, diving if alarmed and swimming some distance underwater. Muskrats usually appear in large numbers wherever they occur, but they are no longer found in Britain.

The **coypu** is considerably larger ▶ than the muskrat. It has webbed hind feet and clawed front feet. Large groups of coypu now live in England and parts of France. They feed on the leaves and stems of waterside plants.

The **brown rat** likes to live within easy ▶ reach of water and is common on the banks of rivers and streams and also around sewers. It is smaller than both the coypu and the muskrat.

Nature ⟋ Notebook

Here are three of the mammals that you may spot by rivers and streams. Keep your eyes open for them when you are out on a riverside walk and colour in the outline as you see each one. Fill in the spaces with your notes.

NAME ___Otter___

DATE _____

PLACE _____

NOTES _____

_____

_____

_____

NAME ___Brown rat___

DATE _____

PLACE _____

NOTES _____

_____

_____

_____

NAME ___Coypu___

DATE _____

PLACE _____

NOTES _____

_____

_____

_____

Picture index

Hare